1/s 8/09
ch 8/10

Baritone/Bass Volume 3
Accompaniment CDs

THE
SINGERS
MUSICAL THEATRE
ANTHOLOGY

A collection of songs from the musical stage, categorized by voice type. The selections are presented in their authentic settings, excerpted from the original vocal scores.

ISBN-13: 978-0-634-06187-5
ISBN-10: 0-634-06187-9

HAL•LEONARD® CORPORATION

7777 W. BLUEMOUND RD. P.O. BOX 13819 MILWAUKEE, WI 53213

Visit Hal Leonard Online at
www.halleonard.com

DISC ONE Track List

BEAUTY AND THE BEAST
- [1] Gaston[1]
- [2] Me[1]
- [3] If I Can't Love Her[1]

CABARET
- [4] Don't Go[3]

CHICAGO
- [5] All I Care About[3]

CLOSER THAN EVER
- [6] If I Sing[5]

THE FIREBRAND OF FLORENCE
- [7] A Rhyme for Angela[1]

FOOTLOOSE
- [8] I Confess[4]

GIGI
- [9] Gigi[3]

THE HAPPY TIME
- [10] I Don't Remember You[5]

I LOVE YOU, YOU'RE PERFECT, NOW CHANGE
- [11] The Baby Song[4]

IS THERE LIFE AFTER HIGH SCHOOL?
- [12] The Kid Inside[5]

JACQUES BREL IS ALIVE AND WELL AND LIVING IN PARIS
- [13] The Bulls[3]
- [14] Funeral Tango[3]

JEKYLL & HYDE
- [15] Lost in the Darkness[1]

THE LITTLE MERMAID (film)
- [16] Les Poissons[2]

MARRY ME A LITTLE
- [17] Happily Ever After[3]

MARTIN GUERRE
- [18] Justice Will Be Done[4]

THE MIKADO
- [19] As Some Day It May Happen[6]

MINNIE'S BOYS
- [20] Mama, a Rainbow[4]
- [21] Where Was I When They Passed Out the Luck?[4]

Pianists on the CDs
- [1] Brian Dean
- [2] Louise Lerch
- [3] Ruben Piirainen
- [4] Christopher Ruck
- [5] Richard Walters
- [6] Laura Ward

DISC TWO Track List

THE MUSIC MAN
  [1] The Sadder but Wiser Girl[1]

NEWSIES (film)
  [2] Santa Fe[5]

ON A CLEAR DAY YOU CAN
  SEE FOREVER
  [3] Come Back to Me[3]
  [4] On a Clear Day
    (You Can See Forever)[3]

ON THE TOWN
  [5] Lucky to Be Me[5]

PARADE
  [6] It's Hard to Speak My Heart[4]

RUTHLESS
  [7] I Hate Musicals[3]

SATURDAY NIGHT
  [8] Isn't It?[1]

SIDE SHOW
  [9] You Should Be Loved[4]
  [10] Private Conversation[1]
  [11] The Devil You Know[4]

SMILE
  [12] Smile[3]

STOP THE WORLD –
  I WANT TO GET OFF
  [13] What Kind of Fool Am I?[5]

SUNSET BOULEVARD
  [14] The Greatest Star of All[1]

TITANIC
  [15] In Every Age[1]
  [16] There She Is[3]

VICTOR/VICTORIA
  [17] King's Dilemma[3]
  [18] Paris by Night[3]

WHEN PIGS FLY
  [19] Sam and Me[4]
  [20] Laughing Matters[1]

WHOOP DEE DOO!
  [21] Last One Picked[3]

Pianists on the CDs

[1] Brian Dean
[2] Louise Lerch
[3] Ruben Piirainen
[4] Christopher Ruck
[5] Richard Walters
[6] Laura Ward

THOUGHTS ABOUT THE ACCOMPANIMENTS AND THE SONGS

We've made every effort to choose a reasonable tempo for the recorded piano accompaniments, based on cast albums or performance precedents. Other tempos could be explored for individual interpretations. We also deliberately attempted to make the accompaniment recordings musically alive, incorporating rubato, ritardandos, accelerandos, and dynamics to inspire a theatrical performance. Nevertheless, by the very nature of recording, ours is ultimately only one interpretation.

In almost all cases we recorded the accompaniments to exactly match the editions printed in *The Singer's Musical Theatre Anthology*. It is important to point out, as a reminder, that the aim of this series is a presentation of theatre literature in its original, unchanged form. Thus, we included the entire song in the printed editions. Very occasionally, when a song felt long for a stand-alone performance or audition, we eliminated a repeat in our accompaniment recording. In those instances a first ending (or D.S.) is omitted, and the accompaniment moves directly to the final ending. For your purposes, you may choose to shorten other songs for live auditions with a pianist. A few words of caution: If this is your intention, mark the score very clearly with your cuts for the audition accompanist.

Ideally, you will be using these recorded accompaniments for practice only. Because the vocal melody is not on the recording by design, you will need to learn this at the piano or another instrument. Or if you don't play well enough to plunk through the melody of a new song, and you don't have a teacher, coach or friend to help you, you may need to seek out a recording. Some words of advice, though: You will come up with a more individual interpretation, conjured from the ground up in the manner in which all the best actors work, if you learn the song on your own, built into your unique singing voice, without imitating a recorded performance.

If you are working on a duet, it is very important that you study not only your own part, but the other singer's part as well. Then you will be ready to handle any missed entrance or mistake that he or she might make in a performance, or any improvisation that comes up, and keep things on an even keel.

Choosing the right song for you and your talents is crucial in theatre music. While all actors want to stretch beyond their "type," it is important for public performances and auditions for you to know what you can do well. There are as many theories about audition literature as there are directors. But all would agree that they want to hear you at your best, not attempting something that for some reason you feel you should do, but is not your strong suit.

There are general vocal guidelines for voice types in theatre music, but these are not in stone. A soprano with a good belt may be able to sing songs from the Soprano volumes as well as the Belter volumes. Belters may work on their "head voice" in Soprano songs. Men who have voices that lie between Tenor and Baritone, commonly called "baritenors," may find songs in both the Tenor and Baritone/Bass volumes. If you have the luxury of being able to transpose music, either through your own abilities or the help of someone else, you might consider taking a song to a different key to suit your voice. Of course, the recorded accompaniments are in only the original show keys, so they won't help you in that situation.

Recording what sometimes seemed like an endless number of piano accompaniments for *The Singer's Musical Theatre Anthology* was a mammoth task. My thanks to the pianists, assistant producers and engineers who worked so graciously with me. I especially thank Brian Dean and Christopher Ruck for their committed and sustained efforts in achieving the finished results.

Surely, with hundreds of songs from a century of shows, in multiple volumes in authentic editions, any singing actor can find several songs for any occasion. Break a leg!

Richard Walters
Series Editor and Producer

ABOUT THE ENHANCED CDs

In addition to piano accompaniments playable on both your CD player and computer, these enhanced CDs also include tempo adjustment and transposition software for computer use only. This software, known as Amazing Slow Downer, was originally created for use in pop music to allow singers and players the freedom to independently adjust both tempo and pitch elements. Because we believe there may be valuable educational use for these features in classical and theatre music, we have included this software as a tool for both the teacher and student. For quick and easy installation instructions of this software, please see below.

In recording a piano accompaniment we necessarily must choose one tempo. Our choice of tempo, phrasing, *ritardandos*, and dynamics is carefully considered. But by the nature of recording, it is only one option.

However, we encourage you to explore your own interpretive ideas, which may differ from our recordings. This new software feature allows you to adjust the tempo up and down without affecting the pitch. Likewise, Amazing Slow Downer allows you to shift pitch up and down without affecting the tempo. We recommend that these new tempo and pitch adjustment features be used with care and insight. Ideally, you will be using these recorded accompaniments and Amazing Slow Downer for practice only.

The audio quality may be somewhat compromised when played through the Amazing Slow Downer. This compromise in quality will not be a factor in playing the CD audio track on a normal CD player or through another audio computer program.

INSTALLATION INSTRUCTIONS:

For Macintosh OS 8, 9 and X:
• Load the CD-ROM into your CD-ROM Drive on your computer.
• Each computer is set up a little differently. Your computer may automatically open the audio CD portion of this enhanced CD and begin to play it.
• To access the CD-ROM features, double-click on the data portion of the CD-ROM
  (which will have the Hal Leonard icon in red and be named as the book).
• Double-click on the "Amazing OS 8 (9 or X)" folder.
• Double-click "Amazing Slow Downer"/"Amazing X PA" to run the software from the CD-ROM,
  or copy this file to your hard disk and run it from there.
• Follow the instructions on-screen to get started. The Amazing Slow Downer should display tempo, pitch and mix bars.
  Click to select your track and adjust pitch or tempo by sliding the appropriate bar to the left or to the right.

For Windows:
• Load the CD-ROM into your CD-ROM Drive on your computer.
• Each computer is set up a little differently. Your computer may automatically open the audio CD portion of this enhanced CD and begin to play it.
• To access the CD-ROM features, click on My Computer then right click on the Drive that you placed the CD in. Click Open. You should then see a folder named "Amazing Slow Downer". Click to open the "Amazing Slow Downer" folder.
• Double-click "setup.exe" to install the software from the CD-ROM to your hard disk. Follow the on-screen instructions to complete installation.
• Go to "Start," "Programs" and find the "Amazing Slow Downer" folder. Go to that folder and select the "Amazing Slow Downer" software.
• Follow the instructions on-screen to get started. The Amazing Slow Downer should display tempo, pitch and mix bars. Click to select your track and adjust pitch or tempo by sliding the appropriate bar to the left or to the right.
• Note: On Windows NT, 2000 and XP, the user should be logged in as the "Administrator" to guarantee access to the CD-ROM drive. Please see the help file for further information.

MINIMUM SYSTEM REQUIREMENTS:

For Macintosh:
Power Macintosh; Mac OS 8.5 or higher; 4 MB Application RAM; 8x Multi-Session CD-ROM drive

For Windows:
Pentium, Celeron or equivalent processor; Windows 95, 98, ME, NT, 2000, XP; 4 MB Application RAM;
8x Multi-Session CD-ROM drive

ANYONE CAN WHISTLE
Everybody Says Don't

BIG RIVER
River in the Rain

CAMELOT
Camelot
C'est Moi
How to Handle a Woman
If Ever I Would Leave You

CAROUSEL
If I Loved You
Soliloquy

CINDERELLA (television)
Ten Minutes Ago
Do I Love You Because You're Beautiful?

COMPANY
Marry Me a Little
Sorry-Grateful

THE FANTASTICKS
Try to Remember

FOLLIES
The Road You Didn't Take

HMS PINAFORE
When I Was a Lad

IOLANTHE
When You're Lying Awake

KISS ME, KATE
Were Thine That Special Face
Where Is the Life that Late I Led?

KNICKERBOCKER HOLIDAY
September Song

LOST IN THE STARS
Lost in the Stars
Thousands of Miles

LOVE LIFE
This Is the Life

MAN OF LA MANCHA
Dulcinea
The Impossible Dream
The Man of La Mancha (I, Don Quixote)

THE MUSIC MAN
Marian the Librarian

OKLAHOMA!
Lonely Room
Oh, What a Beautiful Mornin'

OLIVER!
Reviewing the Situation

PAINT YOUR WAGON
They Call the Wind Maria

THE PIRATES OF PENZANCE
I Am the Very Model

PORGY AND BESS
I Got Plenty O' Nuttin'

SHENANDOAH
I've Heard it All Before
Meditation I
Meditation II

SHOW BOAT
Ol' Man River

SOUTH PACIFIC
Some Enchanted Evening
This Nearly Was Mine

THE THREEPENNY OPERA
Mack the Knife

Also Available
THE SINGER'S MUSICAL THEATRE ANTHOLOGY

Baritone/Bass, Volume 2
Book – HL00747033
Accompaniment CDs – HL00740237

Also Available
THE SINGER'S MUSICAL THEATRE ANTHOLOGY

Baritone/Bass, Volume 4
Book – HL00000396
Accompaniment CDs – HL00000401

ALLEGRO
A Fellow Needs a Girl

ANNIE GET YOUR GUN
I'm a Bad, Bad Man

ASPECTS OF LOVE
Other Pleasures

AVENUE Q
Fantasies Come True
I'm Not Wearing Underwear Today
What Do You Do With a B.A. in English?

BIG RIVER
Waitin' for the Light to Shine

BYE BYE BIRDIE
A Lot of Livin' to Do
Put on a Happy Face

LA CAGE AUX FOLLES
Masculinity

CAMELOT
I Wonder What the King Is Doing Tonight

**ELEGIES FOR ANGELS, PUNKS,
AND RAGING QUEENS**
Heroes All Around

FOLLIES
The Right Girl

**A FUNNY THING HAPPENED ON
THE WAY TO THE FORUM**
Bring Me My Bride

GREASE
Greased Lightnin'

**I LOVE YOU, YOU'RE PERFECT,
NOW CHANGE**
Shouldn't I Be Less in Love with You?

**JOSEPH AND THE AMAZING
TECHINICOLOR® DREAMCOAT**
Those Canaan Days

LOUISIANA PURCHASE
What Chance Have I with Love?

MILK AND HONEY
There's No Reason in the World

MONTY PYTHON'S SPAMALOT
Always Look on the Bright Side of Life

THE MUSIC MAN
Ya Got Trouble

MY FAIR LADY
Get Me to the Church on Time
With a Little Bit of Luck

PAINT YOUR WAGON
Wand'rin' Star

THE PRODUCERS
Along Came Bialy
Haben Sie Gehort Das Deutsche Band?
In Old Bavaria

RAGTIME
Make Them Hear You

THE RINK
Marry Me

**THE ROAR OF THE GREASEPAINT-
THE SMELL OF THE CROWD**
A Wonderful Day Like Today
Who Can I Turn To?

1776
Molasses to Rum

THE SOUND OF MUSIC
Edelweiss

WICKED
Wonderful

THE WILD PARTY
I'll Be Here

WISH YOU WERE HERE
Relax

WOMAN OF THE YEAR
Sometimes a Day Goes By

WONDERFUL TOWN
A Quiet Girl
It's Love

YOU'RE A GOOD MAN, CHARLIE BROWN
The Kite (Charlie Brown's Kite)